D1490802

BENEATH THE SKY
OF AN
ANGRY GOD

John L. Jenkins   Mark W. Weaver

RECONCILIATION PRESS, an imprint of
Trinity Rivers Publishing, Manassas, Virginia

Authors' Note

Our nation's history is like a cord of many strands woven together and twisted so tightly that the strands have become as one. Some strands are good while others are evil. Some speak of the truth while others speak of lies. Some tell of honor, others of treachery. And regardless of the differences in our personal, ethnic or cultural backgrounds, these strands from our nation's past have been woven into our own attitudes and behaviors.

This can be hard for some of us to accept. Human nature wants to place the blame elsewhere, to point the accusing finger at someone besides ourselves. "It's not my fault!" However, when we honestly gaze into the mirror of history, we often see our own reflection in the lives of others and discover that there are no convenient villains.

Using the historical Cherokee Trail of Tears as a backdrop, *Beneath the Sky of An Angry God* dramatizes the trials and the fears of young people who suffered injustice. The Cherokee Trail of Tears is a painful episode in American history when many Americans—politicians and citizens, pastors and congregations—stood by or even participated in what most now agree was a national travesty of justice.

Perhaps we can best learn from this tragedy when we slip into the shoes of those who walked the journey and thus travel a road that has been all but forgotten. We want to inspire both youth and adults not only to learn about our past, but also to use what we learn to become Christ-centered reconcilers in the communities where we live, work and worship.

> *Whatever is has already been, and what will be has been before; and God will call the past into account.*
> (Eccl. 3:15 NIV)

1

STORM CLOUDS

Sixteen-year-old Daniel Sweetwater sat cross-legged on a grassy knoll and clutched a thick, black Bible. Looking left at last, he saw the two plain gravestones bearing the names of his mother and sister.

His dark eyes moved quickly from one name to the next: Rebecca; Sarah. Pain stabbed at his heart, narrowing his eyes and forcing his gaze away from the two gravestones.

His eyes wandered down over the knoll to the two-room cabin where he lived with his father, Thomas. The cabin suddenly looked small compared to the towering black and gray clouds that moved in above.

Daniel lifted his chin. The air smelled like rain.

Seconds later, a flash of lightning speared the earth beyond the creek and hills bordering their cabin. A deafening crack of thunder followed.

Daniel jerked. The storm was close! The churning mass of clouds dwarfed the tiny town of Ellijay which was only about a half-mile away.

Wind snapped Daniel's charcoal black hair across his somber face. He looked upward, setting his jaw firmly and squinting his eyes. He squeezed the Bible.

Why was God angry? Why was He punishing them?

Drops of rain began pelting the ground. As the cool droplets struck and splattered against his face, Daniel thought of his mother. She had died four years earlier—just following a terrible rainstorm.

Daniel could still picture the moment of her death in his mind. Dark clouds crowded the horizon as he and his father had waited on their front porch. Rainwater had pooled around the edges of the porch.

Mrs. Blackcrow, a Cherokee midwife, had opened the front door, shaking her head. Her disheveled white hair hung down in sweaty strands. Her face was as pale as a white man's.

"Thomas, I am sorry," was all she had said.

Daniel and his father's fears had come upon them: both his mother and a new baby sister had died. A stillbirth, Mrs. Blackcrow had called it.

How could four years ago seem so much like yesterday?

Daniel's face dripped with rain and tears. He missed his mother so much, and now even more with trouble so close at hand. He pictured her warm smile. He could almost feel her gentle touch and hear her soft voice calling his name.

He glanced one last time at his mother's and sister's gravestones. What would happen to the graves after he and his father were gone?

Words burst raggedly from his mouth. "Mother, what would you want us to do?"

If only God would allow her to answer! Just this once!

But heaven remained silent, just as it had every day since her death.

In the months that followed, Daniel and his father had learned how to live together without her. But lately their relationship had been one struggle after another.

A lamp flickered in the cabin window below, shifting Daniel's thoughts to his father.

His father expected too much of him. He had higher standards than the other fathers did. And sometimes he didn't let Daniel go out and play with his friends. There were always too many chores to do around the cabin. This only made Daniel more unhappy.

Things were difficult enough without his father's expectations. Though they lived among the Cherokees, Daniel's family belonged to the Delaware tribe. Thomas often told Daniel stories about his great-grandfather, the Delaware Chief Netawatwees.

In the woods of Ohio country in 1776, Chief Netawatwees had

accepted the Christian gospel and had decided to serve the Christian God. He became a pastor and led his tribe into the ways of the Lord. And he took on the Hebrew name Abraham.

Daniel's grandfather, John, had followed in Abraham's footsteps. And now Thomas was the third Delaware in the family line to pastor a Christian flock.

"Son, we are Christians first, then Moravians, then Delaware. The Cherokee people are our mission field. A long time ago, Cherokee tribal leaders came to realize that the white man was not going to stop coming. And so they decided to adopt the white man's ways.

"They wanted to live in peace with the white man. They put down their bows and knives and took up hoes and rakes. They abandoned their stick and mud-daub houses and built homes made of clapboard or brick. They became farmers instead of hunters. Because the Cherokee people wanted to live in peace with the white man, your grandfather left his Ohio homeland to be a part of these people and to bring them the gospel."

Daniel felt that his preacher father sometimes made the townspeople uncomfortable. He had heard the story so many times: the Son of God had come to earth to save mankind; he died on a cross and rose from the dead; he came to give life to all who believe.

Believe? In what?

Wasn't his father's religion really just the religion of the white man? They were men who broke their promises and agreements to satisfy their hunger for lands that were not their own.

Wind gusted across the knoll. Soaked, Daniel glanced up at the swiftly moving clouds bearing down on him. He scowled as a blast of rain slapped his face.

He stood up, with the Bible tucked tightly under his shirt and buckskin jacket. He eyed his cabin and the nearly empty town now covered in the storm's dark shadows.

He dashed down the hill with his questions still unanswered.

2
DEFIANCE

By the time Daniel reached the cabin, the rain fell in torrents. Water poured from the cabin's roof, snaking across the ground in shallow streams. Orange light glowed through the window. Through the rain-soaked glass, Daniel saw the profile of his father's head and shoulders.

Viewing the outline of his father's figure backlit by flame from the fireplace, Daniel could see that his father was reading. His reading glasses hung on the end of his nose.

A faint smile formed on Daniel's face. And for an instant, his heart warmed.

How many times had he come home to this same scene to find his father sitting in the window with his reading glasses perched on the end of his nose?

Sure, they had their differences, but he knew his father loved him. And he loved his father. How could you not love someone so deeply committed to following his own beliefs, someone so dedicated to helping others?

Daniel pushed back the warm feelings. Maybe that was part of the problem. His father cared for others so much that, at times, maybe he forgot what his own son wanted or needed.

Finally, Daniel reached the front porch. Completely drenched, he opened the door and stepped inside. A small pool of water formed quickly at his feet.

"Stayed up there a bit too long, didn't you?" Thomas smiled as he crossed the room and wrapped a blanket around his dripping son. Though forty years old, Thomas' smooth face and wide smile made him appear much younger.

Daniel did not answer as he sloshed toward the fireplace.

"I've just about finished packing," Thomas offered. He waved at one of the open trunks by the foot of their beds.

Daniel ignored him. Pulling up a straight-backed chair, he planted himself firmly, hung his head, and stared resentfully into the fire. His wet black hair hung down over his eyes.

"What's bothering you, son?"

Daniel sulked and stared at the fire. How could his father not know? Everyone in the town of Ellijay had only one thing on their minds: the Cherokee relocation; or, as the white families who steadily poured into their town simply said, "the removal."

He and his father were two in a small remainder who had yet to leave Ellijay, Georgia. The white man's government was determined to move the Cherokees from their homes in Georgia and other nearby states to new homes in a faraway place called Oklahoma.

Daniel did not want to go to Oklahoma. Nobody had wanted to move! But they had no choice. They were being forced at gunpoint!

Daniel sat motionless for several minutes, his anger near boiling. The din of pounding rain on the roof increased. The moisture in his clothes began to rise in pale ribbons of steam.

Their removal brought the same kind of pain to Daniel's heart as sitting on the knoll and looking at his mother's and sister's graves. It was a deep, bitter feeling and at times, like now, the very thought of it made his heart ache uncontrollably.

Daniel jumped to his feet, his anger erupting.

"How can we allow them to do this to us? This is our home! We're no different than they are. We even worship the same God! Isn't that why grandpa left the Delawares and joined the Cherokees to teach them the white man's religion? We're a peaceful people. They're taking our homes, our businesses and our churches to be their own!"

Daniel rose and pulled the Bible free from beneath his shirt. He shook it in the air. "They just can't make us move!"

Thomas walked over to his son. He placed a hand on Daniel's shoulder and looked him in the eye.

"Daniel, we've been over this before. Several years ago, some of our leaders made a treaty with the U.S. government. They and their followers have already moved west."

Stone-faced, Daniel crossed his arms over his chest and stared at his father, then replied. "Some of my friends said they betrayed us."

"Yes, their actions have deeply divided us. But nobody has betrayed us, Daniel. Some of our Cherokee leaders just had the wisdom to see what was coming. Others refused to believe that we would ever have to leave our native homelands.

"Now, General Scott has been appointed to move us. And I've asked God many times what our response should be. Stay, fight and defend our homeland? If we do, we will be destroyed. Or should we give in, save our lives and start again elsewhere?"

Thomas patted his son on the shoulder. "I'm still not sure of God's answer. But I do know this, if there is any hope at all for preserving our rich heritage, we must leave."

"Why did we ever have to come here in the first place?" Daniel lowered his eyes. "We could have just stayed in Hiwassee."

"Son, staying there or moving here would not have made a difference." Thomas' eyes showed compassion and understanding. "The government is moving all the Cherokees, the whole nation—from Hiwassee to Timottee, from Nickojack to Sand Town."

"It's just not—fair," Daniel replied, his voice faltering.

"Son, the land doesn't belong to us. It never really did. The land is God's. It always was and it always will be. No matter who lives here, the land will always belong to God.

"We'll make our new home in the Oklahoma Territory. Everything will be all right. There's nothing that can be done now. Why don't you go lie down and rest? Tomorrow's going to be a long day. We have to be in Fort Gilmer by sundown."

Daniel tossed the Bible toward the table in the center of the room. It landed on the table, then slid and fell to the rough-hewn plank floor.

Then he bolted toward the door and flung it open. "I'm going out!"

He crossed the threshold and stepped into falling sheets of rain, leaving the door ajar.

Thomas stepped over and quickly picked up the Bible. He brushed the cover with his hand as he hurried to the door. He called into the downpour.

But his pleas fell on deaf ears.

3

INTRUDERS

Rain beat on Daniel's back. A chill shot down his spine. He splashed his way to the rear of the cabin, then sprang onto the barrel he used for climbing onto the roof.

He stood up. The edge of the roof came to his chest. Gripping the wood shingles, he pulled himself onto the roof. He then stood and used the chimney to help him work his way to the peak.

Ever since his mother died, the cabin's roof had been Daniel's special place to be alone. It was a place where he could go to think or sometimes talk to God. For a few minutes, he sat tight-lipped with his back to the chimney, eyes staring toward town, ignoring the rain and the threat of lightning.

Then Daniel lifted his face toward heaven.

"God! Why did you allow this removal? You know it's not right! The folks who live in this valley are good people. They love their children; they take care of their elderly. Most of them have even given up their heathen ways. How can you let this happen?"

The torrent continued and matted Daniel's black hair to his head. "I've tried to trust you, God, but every time I decide to put things into your hands, you let me down. First, you took my mother and my sister! Now white men have cheated us out of our town and our homes!"

Daniel pounded his fists against the rough wood shingles until one of his knuckles started to bleed.

"God, I challenge You to be fair! I challenge You to bring justice to these people."

Daniel swallowed hard. "I challenge You to bring justice to my father and to me!"

Movement from the road in front of their property caught

Daniel's eye. At first he could only see a dark, fast-moving knot of men on horseback through the torrential rain. Then the knot broke apart, and three horsemen charged up the rutted lane, kicking clumps of mud and sprays of water behind them. All wore knee-length raincoats and wide-brimmed hats.

Daniel clambered over the roof's peak and slumped down on his knees beside the chimney. Hammering the roof, the rain now mixed with the sound of the hoofs splashing through pools of water lining the lane. The three horsemen drew in their reins and pulled up in front of the cabin. Rain poured from their coats and hats.

The broad-shouldered man in the middle had a bushy, oversized mustache that followed the downward curve of his mouth. He waved his pistol in a sweeping gesture toward the house. He and the man to his right swung their legs over their saddles and dismounted. They handed their reins to the third man who remained on his horse.

Then the two men disappeared beneath the eaves of the roof, their boots thumping loudly on the wooden porch.

The man waiting on his horse looked nervously from side to side, a rifle across his lap.

Daniel ducked down and swung behind the chimney. He shivered as cold rain streamed down his spine.

His thoughts raced wildly. What should he do—could he do?

One thing was sure. He couldn't waste a second!

He worked his way down the backside of the roof. As he neared the edge, he let go and slipped off onto the ground. His feet slid out from under him as he landed on his hands and knees with a loud splat in the mud.

Climbing to his feet, he scrambled around toward the side of the house, his heart pounding.

4

GUNSHOT

Holding his breath, Daniel shot a glance around the corner of the cabin. The lone horseman sat motionless, his collar turned up, his wide-brimmed hat pulled low, and his eyes locked on the front door.

Getting in from here would be impossible!

Daniel crept back along the side to the rear of the cabin, then splashed through the mud to the other side. He would have to risk a look in the window!

With his body pressed against the cabin, Daniel peeked sideways through the window. He saw the back of his father's shoulders and head and the two intruders' scowling faces.

The big man with the broad mustache waved his pistol wildly at Thomas. He snarled as he spoke, but the downpour drowned out whatever he was saying.

His father raised his Bible as a pistol shot barked sharply over the drone of falling rain. His father fell backwards against the hearth. The mustached man's mouth twisted into a half-smile as he holstered his gun and turned toward the door.

A scream caught in Daniel's throat.

His heart nearly exploded in fear as he ran toward the front of the house. As he turned the corner and jumped onto the porch, the three men dug their heels into their mounts and dashed off across the yard toward the road.

Daniel raced through the open door. His father lay crumpled against the hearth, his right hand clutching his left shoulder, his left hand holding the Bible.

Thomas forced a ragged smile and gestured toward the bed. He spoke calmly. "Get the medical kit, Son. It's not as bad as it looks. By God's grace, it's only a flesh wound."

Wide-eyed and speechless, Daniel nodded, then grabbed

the Bible from his father and placed it on the hearth. He dropped to his knees and grabbed the kit from beneath his father's bed.

Daniel cleaned the wound. His father had been right. It could have been much worse. As it was, the bullet had passed clean through the fleshy part of his shoulder, miraculously missing his collarbone and shoulder blade.

Thomas winced with every stroke of salve that Daniel applied to the wound. Then, using two old shirts, Daniel made a dressing. With instructions from his father, he bound the wound and created a sling that wrapped up and around his father's shoulder and pinned his arm to his side. Daniel worked bravely despite the pain creasing his father's face.

Now, only time would tell about the possibility of infection, but by then it might be too late. The town's only doctor was already on his way to the Oklahoma Territory.

When his father was finally resting in his bed, Daniel cleared his throat and spoke up.

"Who were those men, Father? Why did they shoot you?"

"The Crawford brothers. They own all the property around this knoll. They want us off their land."

Daniel's anger surged. "We're leaving tomorrow! Didn't you tell them?"

"They knew." Thomas left the obvious unsaid.

Daniel clenched his teeth and made a fist. "I hate them— I'm going to kill them. I swear I will."

"Son, you'll do no such thing," Thomas chastened. "The Bible teaches us that vengeance is the Lord's. Not ours."

"The man shot you, tried to kill you!" Daniel's eyes flashed. "You can't just let him get away with it!"

Thomas did not flinch at his son's anger.

"God brought us to Ellijay to show the Cherokee people a better way to live. We must prove that the power of the gospel is stronger than the power of the hatred that tempts our hearts."

Daniel edged closer to the fire. "But what about justice?"

Thomas paused to tighten the bandage on his shoulder. He

spoke through a grimace. "The Cherokee have lived on these lands for many generations. Before the white man came, we had our own forms of justice and fairness. Men received punishment for the crimes they committed.

"But now our world has been turned upside down. There is no justice except what the Lord provides. We must forgive and leave matters in God's hands."

Daniel shook, but not from the wet or the cold. "We have a right to this land. You purchased it with hard-earned money. We have to give up land that's worth twenty-five dollars an acre for land that costs the government only a dollar an acre!"

Thomas breathed deeply. "Listen to me now. The few left in Ellijay are the most loyal and determined of our brethren. They refused to believe that the white man would get this land.

"Most of the others have already left. They could see what was happening; they knew it was coming. The people who are left—they need us, son. They need someone to help keep the peace and prevent any more killing. I believe I can do that."

His father's suddenly stern voice made him look up.

"There's one more thing I've got to tell you—why you need to settle your anger. The man who shot me—Jake Crawford—he'll be traveling with us to Oklahoma. He's a Georgia volunteer with the U.S. Army and the federal removal agents."

Daniel turned away from his father. He looked at the Bible on the hearth. Crawford's bullet had drilled a hole directly through the middle—right between the words Holy and Bible.

Daniel slumped onto his bed. Not only had the bullet drilled a hole through the Bible, it had also drilled an even bigger hole through his heart and his faith.

Just what had he and his father and the people of Ellijay done to deserve all of this?

Thunder crashed, booming across the sky above the cabin like the answer of an angry God.

5

WAGONS HO!

Though Jake Crawford's bullet had not struck bone, Thomas could not use his left shoulder or arm. When morning came, he could do little but watch Daniel and the few remaining members of his congregation load the covered wagon with their belongings.

The sun was not yet fully over the horizon when the small wagon train pulled out of Ellijay. Daniel sat on the buckboard and drove the Sweetwater team. Thomas rode beside him, his arm and shoulder wrapped tightly.

As the wagon rambled down the rutted road on the opposite side of the knoll and their cabin, Daniel caught one last glimpse of his mother's and sister's gravestones. The two white stones sat solemn and yet undisturbed, overlooking the cabin and the town which were no longer visible.

Daniel thought once more about all the good times he'd had growing up in Ellijay. And he thought of baby Sarah and how she had never known life at all. With his heart so full of pain, he wondered if maybe she wasn't better off. At least she was in a place where the long-barreled pistols of men like Jake Crawford's could not reach.

Daniel adjusted his straw hat and focused his attention on the road ahead and the eighteen wagons strung out in front of them. They were the last of Ellijay's Cherokee. These proud people had clung to their hopes and dreams until the bitter end. They still could not accept that some of their tribal leaders had agreed to the government's terms.

As their wagon bounced its way further and further from Ellijay, Daniel remembered his father's words and face as he closed the door to their cabin for the final time.

"A new era is about to begin," he had said solemnly.

Daniel frowned. He didn't know about any new era. He only knew his heart felt sad with a sadness so deep that he wondered if it would ever go away.

Rain fell for the whole first day's journey to Fort Gilmer, then continued for the next several days beyond. On the evening of the fourth day, the drenched Ellijay pilgrims rolled into the Cherokee agency camp in Calhoun, Tennessee. They had traveled nearly seventy-five miles. Here the wagon train would link up with other Cherokee tribes from the four states of North Carolina, Tennessee, Alabama and Georgia.

Still driving the wagon, Daniel sat straight up in the buckboard and grabbed his hat. His eyes widened. He had never seen so many wagons and people and soldiers and mud.

Later that evening, with help from the agency's army doctor, Thomas received a new dressing for his arm. Fortunately, his wound was not infected and it had begun to heal. After adjusting his bandages, Thomas regained a little movement and his broad smile returned.

Two days later, the last group of Cherokees arrived and all were made ready for their five-month journey to the Oklahoma Territory. The U.S. Army marshaled over a thousand Cherokees into a long line of wagons, carts and walkers, led in front and followed behind by blue-uniformed U.S. Army soldiers on horseback. They left Calhoun and followed the Hiwassee River westward to where it joined with the Tennessee.

Light rain continued off and on for several more days as the last of the Cherokees to head west forded the rising Tennessee River. They crested Walden's Ridge and headed northwest toward Murfreesboro. The proud but beaten Cherokee people trudged westward, their hopes washed away by the miserable weather.

Daniel cracked the whip on their team of oxen. He pulled up the collar on his deerskin coat and adjusted his broadbrimmed hat. He stared upward at the gray blanket of clouds.

The rain had followed them all the way from Ellijay. He wondered if God would ever let it stop.

Four wagons ahead in the curve of the road, a family struggled to get their wagon out of the mud. Two wagons back, an old full-blood woman wept loudly. She lamented the loss of her home and lands. In the wagon directly behind them, a young child would not stop crying. Sickness had overtaken some in their party even though the journey was less than two weeks old. One of the elderly had already succumbed and been buried in a shallow grave along the westward trail.

Signs of previous Cherokee wagon trains dotted the landscape. Chill, late October winds whistled through skeletons of horses, oxen, cattle and mules marking the wayside. And among the bones, Daniel's sharp eyes found more shallow graves that revealed the final resting places for those in previous wagon trains who had lost their strength to go further.

Late one afternoon after a brief thundershower, Jake Crawford galloped by. His large, speckled horse kicked up mud and flung it against the side of the Sweetwater wagon.

Beneath Jake's open coat, Daniel saw the pistol, the same pistol Jake had used to shoot his father three weeks earlier. From the saddlebag near Jake's leg, hung a long leather boot that bulged with an even more-deadly rifle.

Jake barked out orders as he worked his horse down the muddy trail congested with people and wagons.

"Let's keep these wagons movin'! No time to slow down now! Can't stop for a little rain. I'm warnin' ya—anybody who can't keep up'll be left behind!"

Daniel bristled. He glanced at his father. Thomas' hardened look betrayed his own anger at Crawford's words. As Daniel turned back to the road, he froze on the buckboard and sucked in a breath.

Old Henry Blackcrow knelt in the road, trying to fix a cracked wagon wheel. He never saw Crawford's horse coming. Daniel tried to stand up but could not warn him in time. The horse planted its hoof on Henry's ankle, crushing it into the mud. Henry let out a ragged scream and fell face first against the wagon wheel.

"Oh, dear God!" Thomas exclaimed softly as he reached back into the wagon for the medical kit. "Keep the team under control. I'll do what I can."

Jake Crawford made everyone afraid, and Henry was not the first person to be hurt by Crawford's recklessness. Though the Army's soldiers treated the Cherokees with more respect than Daniel had thought they would, Jake and his hired guns had not, showing little regard for anyone's safety, much less their comfort.

Weeks of dreary skies and showers had made travel difficult enough, and their spirits were low. Now old Henry's ankle was damaged beyond repair. Thomas and a neighbor set the shattered bones as best they could, but there was little they could do to help ease the pain. The injury could be deadly.

They continued on in silence. Thomas sat beside Daniel on the buckboard, his jaw tense, reading his Bible with the hole through the center. He stretched his left arm upward and winced. His weakened shoulder still limited his movement and the dampness gave him additional pain.

"Why don't you get rid of that old Bible?" Daniel questioned. "Jake's bullet ruined it and now he's ruining our lives."

"This Bible was given to me by your grandfather. It was a very special gift and I can't imagine parting with it." Thomas forced a grin. "Besides, there's only a couple of words missing on each page."

Daniel looked away. He was in no mood for his father's attempt at humor.

6

HARLAN SMITH

Near Nashville, Tennessee, the rains finally stopped. Five straight days of early November sun dried the ground and warmed the spirits of the worn travelers. Daniel and his father gathered dry kindling and logs from the nearby woods. They made camp under a sky filled with stars.

Daniel sat cross-legged in front of the fire. His head hung down and his eyelids drooped. To his left, Henry Blackcrow lay covered with a blanket, snoring lightly. He had grown very weak and was near death. Thomas sat nearby and prayed silently, his hand lightly resting on Henry's shoulder.

Thomas looked up. "Henry doesn't want to go on. He's a tired old man. The move has taken a lot out of him. We must trust his soul to God. He doesn't have much time left."

Thomas stood and faced the twenty or so Cherokees who had gathered in a half circle near the fire. He led several hymns and shared from the Bible. He talked about their trials and encouraged everyone to continue in their faith and love. He urged them not to lose hope or yield to discouragement. He asked them to remember how Jesus had suffered unjustly and yet trusted in God's will and care.

Unexpectedly, a voice called from the high grass and darkness off to their right.

"Hello, the fire!"

Thomas paused at the familiar nighttime hail. Every eye turned to him. Would he acknowledge the visitors?

"Come forward!" Thomas replied boldly.

The outline of four horses and two men appeared in the shadows. Everyone around the campfire grew silent.

Thomas stood up. Daniel followed, head forward and eyes peering into the darkness.

The shadowy figures dismounted and tethered their horses. As they approached the campfire, the flickering light revealed two gritty frontiersmen wearing moccasins, knee-length leather coats with thick, upturned collars. Both men had long, bushy beards and fur caps that seemed to blend together at their ears.

Daniel cocked his head to one side.

"Howdy!" the frontiersman exclaimed. "Name's Harlan. Harlan Smith. This here's my partner Jimmy Sanders. Can't deny it, we heard you preachin'. Mind if we join ya? We sure could use a bit o' company 'bout now."

Thomas motioned for the men to sit. Harlan and Jimmy plopped themselves down side by side on a log. Now Daniel could see them both clearly. Both had sparkling blue eyes and honest looks on their weathered faces.

Eyeing Thomas' Bible, Harlan nodded. "When trouble hits hard, readin' outta the Good Book can soothe the soul, 'specially when there ain't no place else to turn. One day the Good Lord's gonna wipe away all yer tears. And mine, too."

Daniel held back a frown. What right did a white man have talking like that!

"You're a student of the Word, then?" Thomas queried, his smile widening.

"Wouldn't call myself a stu-dent," replied Harlan with a smile of his own. He scratched his chin through his beard. "Was kicked outa school early on. Ne'er went back. O'er the years, I done ed-u-cated myself. Always somethin' to learn if'n ya keep yer eyes and ears open."

"Well, you are most welcome here," Thomas offered. "Perhaps you would like to travel with us. We are on our way to the Oklahoma Territory."

Harlan and Jimmy nodded at the same time, but it was Harlan who spoke.

"That's kindly of ya', but we're just trappers an' hunters, travelin' from Missouri country all the way to the Carolinas and back. Shot us a couple o' bucks an' some turkey. Ain't had a chance to smoke 'em yet. They're gonna be spoilt if they don't be eaten. Thought maybe you'd be hungry. This here trail's been home to many a hungry and proud Cherokee these last few years."

Daniel leaned forward. Maybe he had judged the frontiersman too quickly.

Harlan looked around the group before continuing. "Now, I hope you ain't worryin' about ol' Jimmy and me. Why don't ya just have one of yer men go an' pull that buck from Jimmy's pack horse. An evenin' with kindly folks like you's mor'n worth eighty pound of good ven-i-son.

"Besides, thirty years on the frontier has a way of teachin' a man somethin' about hisself and how to treat others. Most men really ain't lookin' to hurt nobody, and the one's who do are gonna pay fer it in the end. Lake of fire—that's what the Book says, anyway."

Daniel's ears perked up. He smiled and thought of Jake Crawford in a boiling pool of brimstone and sulfur.

"Listen," Harlan continued, his eyes darting to Daniel. "I seen a lot a death along this trail. Been ridin' up and down this road some fourteen years now. Seen whites killin' Injuns, Injuns killin' whites. Whites killin' whites and Injuns killin' Injuns! Seen black men runnin'. Seen white men chasin' black men. Seen all kinds o' people raidin' an' lootin'. All the same—people's people. Some's good and some's bad. Don't make no difference what color their skin if they got hate burnin' inside 'em."

Daniel tensed. All his life, he had lived with his own Indian brothers. Although many of Ellijay's townspeople were half-bloods, the only full-blooded white men he had ever seen were men like Jake Crawford, or others almost as bad.

Thomas nodded. "Sounds to me like you've got the beginnings of a fine sermon."

"Lord knows, I ain't no preacher! It's jes that livin' on the frontier drives a man to choose which way he'll go—good or bad. If to good, you'll be a wiser, better man. If to bad, you'll end up killin' before it's over."

Daniel folded his arms over his knees, his eyes wide open and fixed on Harlan.

"My Ma and Pa left Penn-syl-vanee and headed to western Illinois in '98. I was only four years old. Never got there though. Least not my folks. Somewhere on the trail—don't know where 'cause I was so little—we was attacked by a band of Injuns. They just came up over the hill a whoopin' an' a hollerin'. Didn't know what hit us. I think they was Shawnee, but I ain't sure.

"Ma and Pa got kilt. I was back with Uncle Billy—Jimmy's daddy. After lucky shots dropped three Injuns, they broke off their attack. Jimmy's family was the only one that made it. After that, they buried my folks an' took me in. That's why me an' Jimmy's like brothers. Been together forty years."

Harlan looked over at Jimmy and winked. Jimmy grinned back.

"Well, after that happened to my folks, I hated Injuns. Hated 'em bad. Kilt a couple, too. Wish now that I hadn't, but I did. Cain't fix it, though I would if I could.

"Then somethin' happened one day that changed all that. Yes sir, changed it all!"

7

HARLAN'S STORY

Harlan stretched out his legs and rubbed his knees. His deerskin trousers were worn and scarred from life in the rough.

"I'd been trappin' alone fer a couple a weeks, deep in the Caintuckee woods. The cold set in and snow covered the ground. I tethered my horse and went to set a trap. Got careless. The trap sprung and caught my right arm. Right here—" Harlan gripped the middle of his forearm. "Couldn't get it out, no matter how I worked it.

"And with my rifle strapped to my horse and my horse tied to a tree, well I was sorely in trouble. Trapped I was. Jes' like an old bear. Nobody around fer miles. Those iron teeth had cut into my arm real bad. Blood was all over the place. I said to myself, 'Harlan Smith, you're a goner for sure!' Seen it once and it weren't pretty, when a man was so stupid as to get hisself trapped by his own trap!

"So I laid there all day waitin' to die—that or cut off my own arm with my huntin' knife and then bleed to death! As it was, my arm'd got all clotted up and stopped bleedin'.

"Well, by evenin' I was mighty hungry. I started wonderin' when the good Lord was gonna take me."

Harlan paused for effect. He looked around the circle of quiet, fire-lit faces. "You can bet I done some business with God.

"You might guess that come next morning I woke as hungry as that bear I was tryin' to trap. The dried beef and trail biscuits in my saddlebag were on my mind, but when I opened my eyes, I found me an Injun standin' less than ten feet away. He was all by hisself.

"He was lookin' at me like he didn't know what to do. Didn't say nothin', just stood there an' watched. I tried to talk to him.

He didn't know what I was sayin', I suppose. If he did, he ne'er said a word.

" 'Sides havin' my arm in a trap, I was cold and this Injun knew it. He built a fire. Not too close, mind ya. Just close enough fer me to get a bit o' heat. Barely kep me from freezin'. Figured he was teasin' me before he took my horse and left me to die.

"Now the whole day passed. I tried talkin' to him over and again, but he paid never a mind to me. He just sat there, wooden-faced, wrapped up tight in a fine, red-brown fur cloak made from fox pelts. I suppose he was decid'n what he should do.

"The fire was almost died out and the sun was a startin' to set when this feller just got up an' left. I hollered at him, but he just kep walkin' straight on into them woods. Didn't touch my horse though. Or my saddlebag.

"Bein' somewhat con-fused, I just laid there sayin' my prayers. As dark was settlin' in, I looked up an' he was back ag'in and with a big ole turkey slung acrost his back.

"He got the fire goin ag'in an' built a spit over it. Skewed that turkey an' started it a cookin'. This time the fire was bigger an' I got warmed up just a little more. Never mind my arm was still mashed between a mean set of iron teeth.

"But I was o' so mighty hungry. With nothin' to fill me fer two days, I was gettin' weak, too. Now ya can imagine that I was a hopin' he'd give me somethin' to eat. And let me tell ya, that bird smelt better'n anythin' I'd e'er smelt.

"Then that Injun jumped up and walked to my horse, reached in my boot an' pulled out my rifle. I remember just shaking my head. If a man's a gonna kill ya, at least he oughta have the decency to feed ya first. There's nothin' worse than dyin' on an empty stomach.

"Rifle in hand he came and stood over me. I thought to myself now this is surely it, Harlan. I just looked him in the eye and quietly said, 'Get ready Lord 'cause here I come.' "

Harlan rubbed his jaw and then smiled.

"He lowered the rifle. I musta been a pitiful sight 'cause at the last I closed my eyes. He pulled the trigger and the gun went off. Next thing I knew the spring latch flew off the trap and those iron teeth were layin' open on the ground. When I looked up, he was a puttin' the rifle back in its boot.

"I looked at my arm. Not as bad as I thought. Still got scars though." Harlan pulled up the sleeve to his coat and showed everyone the row of red teeth-marks dotting his forearm.

"So, anyways, by then that Injun' was back over to the fire. I didn't know what to say. While I was shufflin' to my feet, he pult a leather sheath from his belt, drew out a knife and buried it in that there bird.

"Then he pointed his finger at the turkey, dropped the sheath an' disappeared into the woods."

Harlan glanced around the circle of faces a second time, stopping at Daniel.

"Like I says before, some people's good an' some's bad. Ya cain't never judge a man's heart by the color of the skin on his face or the clothes he wears.

"Sooner or later, somethin' in all our hearts just goes wrong—somethin' only God can fix. Sin ain't no re-spec-ter of persons, no sir-ee. And this here country just seems to bring out the best and worst in folks.

"Ain't the way God intended it. He gave us a great land. It's big. Oughta be plenty o' space fer ever'body. We need to keep prayin' that God Almighty helps us find a way to live together."

Harlan looked at Thomas. "Well that's my story."

Thomas smiled. "That was a powerful testimony, my friend."

The informal service concluded with a hymn and a few prayers for understanding among the white men and red men. After the meeting was officially finished, Harlan and Jimmy helped divide the buck so everyone had a fair share of meat. The meat was cut into strips and left to smoke throughout the night.

After more chatter and laughter, Thomas and Daniel finally

said good night to everyone and turned in. Harlan and Jimmy made camp near the Sweetwater wagon. Harlan volunteered to take the first watch.

Daniel had never heard a story like the old frontiersman's. Daniel lay on his back and looked up at the starlit sky. The rains had finally stopped. The ground had finally begun to dry. And the occasional smell of smoke reminded him that they would enjoy several days of venison. A smile slowly crept across his face.

All grew quiet in the camp. Daniel noticed the sounds of the forest. They played like sweet music in his ears. Where was he? Somewhere between Ellijay and the Oklahoma Territory. Somewhere deep in the mountains of Tennessee.

For sure, Daniel knew he was between two worlds: the small world of Ellijay that he had known and a world he did not yet know. He took a deep breath and rolled over on his side. His eyelids grew heavy as he rolled Harlan's story over again in his mind.

A deep, unexpected peace washed over his soul. For the first time in what seemed like months, Daniel felt hope in his heart. Maybe his father had been right. Maybe this was the beginning of a new era. If there were other men like Harlan, white men and Indians just might find a way to get along.

A few moments later, Daniel drifted off into a deep rest like no sleep he had known in a long, long time.

8

STALE BREAD

The next morning, Harlan and Jimmy could not be found. They left no trace of their visit from the night before except for the venison smoking over the coals and the words that remained in the hearts and minds of everyone who had heard Harlan's story.

In the gray light of dawn, Daniel picked up his bedroll, then froze. Lying on the ground was a leather-sheathed knife. He ran to the wagon and stuffed the bedroll in the back.

He returned to the knife and knelt down. Where had it come from? Then Harlan's story came back to him. Could it really be the knife the Indian left Harlan? And why would he leave it with Daniel?

The questions were many, but Daniel's decision was simple. After spying his father's legs and boots resting motionless on the buckboard with the rest of him blocked by the wagon's fabric cover, Daniel snatched up the knife. He returned to the wagon and quickly stowed it away in the trunk with his personal belongings.

Before the sun was fully up, the wagon train formed again. Their journey continued with the weather unseasonably warm and dry. Spirits were lighter, and Jake Crawford had not been seen in their section of the train for several days.

Afternoons grew shorter. One evening a week later, the train broke for camp early. Everyone, including the U.S. Army horsemen, was especially tired that night from their climb up to the Cumberland Plateau. After dinner, when all were settled into their groups and stories were being swapped around the fire, a full moon lit the sky and the stars shone with exceptional brightness.

Daniel stood by the wagon, watching his father on his blanket as he read by the fire. Then Daniel reached into his trunk and brought out the leather-sheathed knife. He brooded, wondering what his father would say about it. But the risk of disapproval was not as strong as his desire to wear and use it.

Daniel closed his hand around the knife, then returned to the blanket beside his father.

Thomas finally noticed Daniel holding the knife. "Where'd you get the knife, son?"

"Found it beneath my bedding the morning Harlan left."

"Can I see it?" Thomas asked. Daniel handed it to him.

Studying the tooled leather, Thomas' eyes brimmed suddenly with tears.

Daniel leaned forward. "What's wrong?"

Thomas set his Bible on the blanket. He slowly turned the sheath over and over in his hand.

"Son, I've told you about your great-grandfather Abraham, how he came to know the Lord Jesus Christ, how he led the Delaware tribe into the way of salvation."

"Yes, I know that story."

Picking up the sheath, Thomas turned it over in his hand. "This sheath and knife belonged to a Delaware warrior."

Daniel made the connection. "A Delaware saved Harlan?"

"I think so, Son. Just seeing this brings some of your grandfather's stories to mind—"

The sound of a pistol shot cut off Thomas' words.

Both father and son looked up as a frightened old Cherokee lumbered past, clutching an object close to his chest. It was Robert from Ellijay and he was obviously drunk!

Daniel jumped to his feet. Hoofbeats followed.

Jake Crawford thundered by, his horse spraying dirt onto the Sweetwaters' blanket. Jake laughed loudly as he closed swiftly on his prey.

Thomas joined his son and started down the trail. Daniel quickly strapped the sheath to his belt. They followed along as Jake, still mounted, snagged the old Cherokee by the collar and dragged him back toward camp, hollering and kicking.

As Jake passed by them, the old man dropped what he was

clutching to his chest. Daniel bent over and picked up half a loaf of stale bread; then, they continued on past a dozen wagons until they found a semicircle of Army wagons surrounding a large campfire.

A large crowd of Cherokees had gathered. Daniel and Thomas edged their way to the front. As he and his father broke into the open circle and faced the group of soldiers, Jake pointed his finger toward Daniel and bellowed.

"And there's the evidence! Stolen supplies."

Daniel's eyes grew wide and his heart beat faster. He looked at the torn loaf of bread he was holding.

Jake strode across the opening to Daniel. He snatched the loaf of bread out of his hand. Jake's pale eyes flashed evilly. "Thanks boy, you just made my job a whole lot easier."

Daniel felt so foolish. He looked closely at Jake Crawford, face to face. Jake's large, husky frame, square jaw, down-turned mustache and cold stare made him even more terrifying up close than he was on horseback.

"You're charging Robert Muskrat for stealing an old loaf of bread?" Thomas asked calmly, stepping forward.

"This don't concern you." Jake growled and waved his arm. "We've got to keep this wagon train under control. When someone steals, he's gonna get punished!"

Jake moved across the circle and talked to the soldiers in hushed tones. More Cherokees continued to gather around the campfire as the soldiers shook their heads and walked away from the circle and into the darkness down the trail.

A minute later, Jake Crawford turned back to face the group. "I'm going to make an example of him! Can't have this kinda thing goin' on in my part of the wagon train!"

Two of Jake's men appeared from behind a wagon with old Robert Muskrat in tow, his feet dragging across the ground. They tied him to the wagon wheel, his back to the campfire.

With one hand, Jake ripped the shirt from Robert's back. In his other hand, Jake held a bullwhip. He uncoiled and snapped it in the air. The leathery crack made everyone flinch.

Old Robert howled even before Jake's first stroke tore across his back. Jake, his brawny frame arching and snapping the whip with great force, began to thrash the old Cherokee. Daniel groaned and winced at the sounds of leather smacking flesh and of Robert's desperate cries. The crowd stood stunned. No one knew quite what to do.

Thomas crossed the circle to the wagon where Jake was unleashing his fury. Daniel could not hear what his father said.

Flicking the tip of the whip back and forth along the ground, Jake stopped and stared angrily at Thomas. Jake guffawed and pushed Thomas to the ground.

"Get on outa here, before I take the whip to your back."

His eyes filling with tears, Thomas stepped back into the crowd as Jake returned his attention to Robert. His whip continued to cut stripes into the Cherokee's back until the old man slumped unconscious to the ground. Jake cut the ropes holding the old man's arms and Robert tumbled backward to the ground.

Thomas, with Robert's two brothers, rushed to the old man's side. The rest of the crowd slowly dispersed to their wagons beneath Jake Crawford's withering glare.

Thomas turned to Daniel. "We need to move him. There's nothing we can do for him here."

After helping Robert back to his wagon and cleaning his wounds, they left him in the care of his brothers. On their way back down the trail, they passed Jake's wagon. He and his men were singing loudly and telling jokes.

Daniel and Thomas wearily returned to their wagon and blankets. Drained of emotion, neither wanted to talk.

Daniel frowned and pulled a clump of dirt from under his head, the same clump that Jake's horse had kicked up a half-hour before. He leaned back on his elbows and stared into the low-burning fire.

Even though bright stars and a full moon filled the sky, darkening storm clouds began to crowd their way back around his heart.

9

CONFRONTATION

Daniel trudged along slowly behind the Sweetwater wagon. The late November sun tried to warm the cold morning air. The colors and fullness of autumn seen at the beginning of their journey had now become brown and barren.

Thousands of Cherokee pilgrims had traveled this trail in the last few years. Today, Thomas drove the wagon that brought up the rear of the wagon train bound for Oklahoma Territory, the very last Cherokee wagon to travel this mountainous trail.

The few Cherokees who had refused to leave not only Ellijay but also other Cherokee towns, would slowly die or, if allowed, be absorbed into other tribes. They would fade into the wilderness, never to be heard from again. They would marry into the poor families that were moving into the Appalachian region. Their Cherokee blood would mingle with white men's blood. And in a few generations, they would almost forget that they ever were once a part of the proud Cherokee people.

To the left of the trail, unmarked gravestones poked out of the ground. Daniel thought of his friend Robert Muskrat and fingered the worn leather sheath strapped to his belt.

Robert Muskrat died two days after his brutal whipping. At the grave site, Thomas placed his hands on Daniel's shoulder and said, "Son, you are becoming a man. Soon you'll have to decide which way you will go in life. I encourage you to reflect on the words of Harlan Smith. He was a wise man."

Daniel remembered Harlan's nearly toothless grin and his awkward mannerisms. A warm feeling started to return. Harlan was the first white man Daniel had ever liked. He pictured the campfire and the scraggly faced old frontiersman bobbing and weaving. He recalled Harlan's dancing eyes.

But now Harlan's words came back to mock him, how a

man had to choose which way to go: "If to good, you'll be a wiser, better man. If to bad, you'll end up killin' before it's over."

Daniel took a deep breath and rubbed his palm over the knife's handle. How could you defeat an evil man like Crawford by doing good? His father said forgiveness brought healing and that hatred only brought trouble.

"I'll never forgive Jake Crawford! Not for all the evil he's done!" The angry words exploded from Daniel's lips.

A horse's whinny, followed by a man's mocking laughter, split the air.

Startled, Daniel spun to his left.

Crawford pulled on his horse's reins and slowed to a stop in the thick grass alongside the Sweetwater wagon.

"Didn't hear me comin', did you? You stupid little savage!" Crawford sniggered, throwing back his head. "I don't need forgiveness from nobody. Especially, you! This is a white man's world, boy. And you better stay out of my way, or you'll end up by the wayside like the others!"

The Sweetwater wagon pulled to the side and stopped. Thomas climbed down and stepped resolutely toward Crawford. Daniel had never seen so much fire in his father's eyes.

"Jake, this is not your world, it's God's world!"

Daniel studied Crawford's hateful, glaring eyes. They looked as if they would pierce his father's soul.

But his father did not back down. "One day, God will have his way with you, Jake Crawford."

Words tried to form on Crawford's lips, but they would not come. His mustache twitched as he sat paralyzed for several long seconds. With a gurgle in his throat, Crawford dug his spurs into his steed's sides.

Then without a single word, he yanked his horse around and headed toward the front of the wagon train.

Thomas climbed back onto the buckboard and snapped the reins. The wagon lurched forward.

Daniel began walking again, his legs weak, his arms heavy and Crawford's threats ringing in his ears.

The sluggish wagon train continued westward across the wooded hills of central Tennessee. Daniel and Thomas' wagon, still near the end of the rambling string of dispossessed Cherokees, stopped for a moment at the crest of one of the hills. Below, miles and miles of forest stretched out before them.

And through the tree-lined trail, Daniel saw portions of a two-mile-long wagon train creeping down into the valley. A low, gray mountain range rose in the distance. A sparkling river split the valley. White billowy clouds swept across a pale blue sky.

Daniel had never felt so small. He stood beneath the big sky and thought for a moment about the Great Spirit. That's what his people had called God. Could his father's God, the Christian God, deliver them from evil any better than the Great Spirit?

The westward lands before him seemed vast, the sky bigger than it had ever been in Ellijay or Hiwassee. He hitched up his trousers and sighed. With every passing mile, he realized the life he had known would never be the same.

As the month neared its end, the air grew colder, and more than once, a light snow dusted the ground. Then, on the first day of December, just north of the Kentucky border, the Ellijay group came upon two disabled wagons near the intersection of two trails. Thomas and Daniel stopped to help.

Peter and Virginia Muhlenberg were Moravian missionaries who, with their children Margaret, Mary and Edward, were on their way from Kentucky to the Shawnee Mission in Kansas. Virginia's sister Hilda and her four year-old son, Jonathan, accompanied them. It was Virginia's wagon wheel that had broken.

Jake Crawford galloped up. "What's the problem?"

"Broken wheel," Thomas replied as he crouched beside the axle. Daniel backed several paces away.

"I can see that!" Crawford sneered, ignoring Thomas as he slipped down from his horse.

Crawford removed his hat and sauntered toward the Muhlenbergs. "How can we help you folks?" he politely inquired, repeatedly eyeing their heavily loaded wagons.

Daniel did not like the hungry look in Crawford's eyes.

Peter Muhlenberg stepped forward, offered his hand to Crawford and introduced his family. He explained the situation.

"We'd be mighty glad to have you folks join us," Jake offered with a broad sweep of his hat. "You'd be much safer traveling with us, that is, if you don't mind the company."

Crawford looked down his nose at Daniel and Thomas.

The Muhlenbergs thanked Crawford as he remounted his horse. Several Ellijay parishioners had already set up a makeshift lever to raise the wagon off the ground.

Crawford sat for a moment and fixed his gaze on Thomas, already working to repair the broken wheel. "Help these people. They'll be traveling with you."

With a nod of his head to the Muhlenberg family, Crawford rode off.

10
NEW FRIENDS

The presence of new people cheered everyone but Daniel. His heart, cold and unforgiving, could not see beyond their white faces. Even after several days, he still refused to speak to Margaret and her younger sister Mary, though Margaret was near his own age.

But Margaret proved very persistent, unlike any girl Daniel had ever met. The following Sunday morning as Thomas and Peter called the people together for a meeting, she stopped him by the corner of a wagon. With hands on her hips and determination in her brown eyes, she proclaimed, "I don't care if you like me or not, Daniel Sweetwater! I'll be friends with whomever I want—including you!"

After several more days of his cold shoulder, she finally found a way to penetrate his hard exterior. "I'm going fishing, Daniel Sweetwater. You can come if you want to."

That evening, after the wagon train closed ranks, Daniel found himself sitting on the riverbank next to Margaret, fishing poles in their hands. They talked for hours.

Margaret explained her parents' missionary work.

"We have always lived with native tribes, Daniel. God called my parents many years ago to serve the Shawnee, the Creek, the Cherokee, the Delaware.

"Your people are losing their lands—it's not going to stop. You know that. My people will keep coming. As long as there is land, they'll keep coming. There's not much we can do."

Margaret paused, then looked straight at Daniel. "And as long as my people keep coming, your people will have to keep moving west. So we keep moving, too. You'll find that we're not fair-weather friends as some are. Our next home will be in Shawnee Mission. My father will pastor there."

Margaret's words made Daniel feel angry inside. Still, he liked Margaret. He liked her a lot. And he knew she spoke the truth. The East now belonged to the white man.

That evening, the Muhlenbergs invited the Sweetwaters for dinner. Daniel relaxed just a little bit, and Thomas told Peter Muhlenberg how happy he was that his son had found a new friend.

The dinner, a rare spread of fresh venison, boiled carrots and Mrs. Muhlenberg's best biscuits, satisfied Daniel's appetite like no meal he'd had in many months.

After dinner, Margaret's eyes sparkled with a hint of mischief.

She said to Daniel. "Stay here. I've got something for you. I'll be right back."

She darted off to her wagon. In less than a minute, she appeared again, holding her hands behind her back. "I've got a gift for you, Daniel Sweetwater."

Daniel grinned widely. Why he liked Margaret, he wasn't sure. White people were not to be trusted. They always brought trouble. But for some reason, he found himself enjoying her and her family. Even little Mary. Both she and Margaret treated him like a brother.

"What is it?" he asked.

"I can't tell you. It's a surprise. You have to stand up and close your eyes."

Daniel stood. "I'm not too sure about this."

Daniel felt Margaret draw near. He could smell the scent of soap in her hair.

She stood face to face with him, extended her arms and began to place something on his head. He instinctively reached up and grabbed it from her. His now opened eyes grew wide with unexpected joy.

"A new hat! Where'd you get that?" Suddenly aware that all eyes were on him, he hung his head and made a sheepish grin. He could hardly believe that she had actually paid attention when he'd lost his hat in the wind over a week ago.

"Thank you. But where I got that hat is my business, Daniel Sweetwater."

Suddenly, in the midst of their fun, a crack of thunder shattered the festive twilight air. Everyone broke quickly for their wagons.

That night after the rain stopped, Daniel lay on his back, thinking about Harlan Smith and the Muhlenberg family. Maybe there were good white people after all. He rolled over on his side, his heart at rest and his thoughts on Margaret.

Above him, the clouds momentarily parted. The moon and the stars came briefly into view, casting their silvery light on his smiling face.

11

THE RIVER

The rains fell heavily all night and most of the next day. By late afternoon, they slowed to a drizzle again. The train made little progress.

Shortly before sunset, the last quarter mile of wagons reached the Red River crossing. The water was rising rapidly and would soon overflow its banks.

"Let's go! Got to get across before dark. Get these wagons moving!" Crawford barked.

Three soldiers approached Crawford near the riverbank. Daniel saw Jake shaking his head forcefully, then motioning with his arms toward the river. After a few moments of animated conversation, the soldiers walked back up the hill. Crawford had gotten his way. He refused to allow the river and the night to divide the wagon train.

The wagons began to roll as the drizzle abruptly turned to rain. Tall dark clouds began to spill long plumes of water trailing across the charcoal sky. One wagon after another rumbled down the grassy bank and into the wide river. Jonathan Aycock, a half-blood, and his full-blood wife, Little Bird, refused to enter the flow. Crawford pulled out his whip and struck Aycock's horses until they moved into the water.

Thomas piloted the Sweetwater wagon safely to the other side. The Muhlenbergs forded successfully right behind him, but the river was already rising quickly. Only the wagon belonging to Virginia's sister Hilda remained on the far bank.

Daniel watched small branches and clumps of dead leaves whisk downstream. He shook his head and wondered why the soldiers had allowed Jake to attempt the crossing.

Hilda and Jonathan followed with George Little Trees commanding the reins. George was one of Thomas' faithful parishioners, a man who had lost his wife to bilious fever just three weeks before. Thomas and the Muhlenbergs prayed silently from the opposite bank as Hilda's wagon entered the rushing waters.

Two-thirds of the way across, the wagon stalled. George stood up and snapped the reins. Leaning away from George, Hilda wrapped one arm around Jonathan and gripped the buckboard with her free hand. The horses struggled as the river splashed up against their shoulders. Still the wagon would not budge.

Daniel shuddered. He had never seen a river run so swiftly!

Without hesitation, Thomas handed Daniel the reins. He lept down and unhitched his team of oxen and led them to the edge of the river. He waded in until he was waist deep, approaching Hilda's team of horses. He secured his harness to hers and waded further in toward the wagon, holding on to the horses until he was chest deep in the water.

Sudden movement caught Daniel's eye. A slanting gray wall of falling rain ran along the river. A downpour was upon them!

And with a glance further upstream, he saw a two-foot wave racing toward them—and riding the wave was a large uprooted tree!

"Father! Lookout!" he shouted, his hands cupped over his mouth.

Thomas turned at Daniel's cry, his eyes moving to the wave and the careening log. Fear rippled across his face.

But only for an instant. Thomas grabbed the edge of the buckboard and tore himself from the swirling torrents around the wagon.

Standing on a wagon wheel, he grabbed Hilda's already-frightened son around the waist and in one motion, threw the terrified child toward one of the soldiers wading in the river near the horse team.

Hilda screamed. Thomas grabbed for the buckboard, but could not hold on.

Twisting and turning in the roiling waters, the tree, like a giant spear, slammed into the faltering wagon. The crackling sound of crushing timber split the air as the tree impaled the wagon.

The wagon tipped sideways. Hilda and George cried out, lost their balance and fell into the water. Thomas, stretching with all of his might to reach Hilda, was instantly swept from sight.

The blow ripped the wagon away from the team of oxen and horses. Loosed from the wagon, the heavier oxen struggled to keep their heads above water and lumbered toward the bank and safety. The horses, however, lost their footing in the high, fast-moving river. Snorting and struggling, tangled in their harnesses, the current swept them down river still hitched to each other.

In the terrible confusion of frantic motion and sounds, Daniel could not see or hear his father.

He leapt from his buckboard to the muddy riverbank as Hilda's wagon toppled onto its side, breaking up into several pieces. Trunks and crates, wagon wheels, clothing, the wagon's cover, and loose wooden planks all swept past the horrified onlookers. The soldier with Hilda's son clung to a rope tossed down from a group of men shouting from the bank. Women shrieked.

Daniel ran toward the raging water.

"Father! Father!" he yelled, hoping against hope to see his father reappear.

Three Cherokees leapt bareback onto their horses and tore down the riverbank. They searched for any sign of Thomas, Hilda and George. Two soldiers mounted their horses and joined in the search.

Half a mile away, the river narrowed as it ran around a bend and into a thick forest. By now, the riders were far ahead of Daniel. Daniel ran with recklessness, his frightened eyes searching the riverbanks. He slipped and fell on the wet grass, stumbling forward into a thorn bush that ripped back the skin from the corner of his right eye. He jumped up and continued running, looking for any place where his father or the others might have grabbed onto a rock, a branch, or a tree.

Just before the river rounded the bend, the horses were found, their harnesses twisted around the branches of a partially submerged tree, their lifeless bodies buffeted in the churning water.

The search party dashed into the forest as the sky darkened, reappearing just as Daniel reached the forest's edge. One of the Cherokees dismounted and grabbed him around the shoulders.

Daniel twisted, trying to break free, but further search was useless in the dark. After much coaxing, Daniel returned to camp, exhausted and covered from head to foot in mud. Blood trickled down the side of his face from the deep scratch near his right eye.

The cloudy sky blackened.

Crawford and his men rode the line and signaled the end of the day. The rains slowed. Few words were spoken as weary families settled in for the night.

After a cold supper and a time of sober prayer, Peter, Virginia, Mary and Edward turned in, taking their now motherless nephew, Jonathan, to bed with them.

Margaret and Daniel, wrapped in blankets, sat on opposite sides of the fire in the silent darkness. Earlier, she had washed and salved the gash near his eye. The wound was clean.

"You really loved your father, Daniel."

Daniel did not respond. Instead he stared upwards into the moonless, starless night. His father—a Delaware Indian with the white man's religion and pastoring a church full of Cherokees. What kind of world had his father brought him into? What kind of man was his father anyway? Daniel had never considered this question. He had always been too angry, too focused on himself to really pay close attention to the things his father had tried to teach him.

Loved his father? Grief stabbed suddenly at his heart—of course he loved his father! If only he had taken the opportunity to tell him more often. Now that opportunity was gone.

A horse and rider approached. Daniel lifted his head and stiffened. Jake Crawford dismounted, removed his hat and held it close to his broad chest.

Daniel reached under the blanket and edged his knife from its sheath. The memory of his father's hands slipping from Hilda's tipping wagon sliced into his thoughts. If only Crawford hadn't shot his father through the shoulder back in Ellijay, maybe he would have been strong enough to have made it out of the river.

Jake sauntered over to where the two were seated. "I'm real sorry 'bout your aunt, Miss Muhlenberg. If there's anything I can do, please let me know."

He glanced down at Daniel but said nothing. He looked back at Margaret, nodded, then turned and walked away.

Daniel stared icily at Jake's back, his hand gripping the knife tightly. Out of the corner of his eyes, he could see Margaret's eyes drop to the blanket. Had she seen the tip of the knife reflecting the campfire's glow?

Crawford mounted his horse and rode away.

Steely-eyed, Daniel slid his knife back into the sheath. Shifting in his blanket, he turned his back on the fire and faced the darkness of the night beneath the sky of an angry God.

12

INJUSTICE

The Cherokee Trail of Tears stretched for nearly one thousand miles. The weary band had traveled from central Georgia, through the mountains of Tennessee and Kentucky, and across central Missouri. Daniel and his friends had made it three-fourths of the way to their destination in the Oklahoma Territory.

Nearly one out of ten from the original group had died along the trail. His father, Hilda, and George had now been added to that list. Early the following morning after the flash flood, one of Thomas' boots, Hilda's shawl and several pieces of George's clothing had been recovered further downstream near a place where the river tumbled into a narrow, rocky gorge. Their bodies had not been found. Small piles of rocks and wooden markers bearing their names were now part of the removal's bitter legacy.

Now a month later with these sad thoughts in mind, Daniel Sweetwater folded his blanket and placed it on the buckboard. Breakfast was finished and it was time for the wagons to roll again. He turned around, looking west down the trail to see if movement had begun.

Margaret helped her father extinguish the fire and then walked back to Daniel's wagon. Since his father's drowning in the Red River, Margaret had been riding with Daniel almost every day.

"Where's that smoke coming from?" he asked her.

Margaret turned around to see. "I don't know, Daniel. It looks too big to be a campfire."

They climbed onto the buckboard and awaited the signal to move. A chill winter wind knifed across the trail. Daniel adjusted his coat collar and tightened his scarf. Margaret pulled a blanket snugly around her. She slid across the seat closer to him.

A few minutes after the wagons began to roll, William Dawes, the Cherokee in charge of the supply wagon, came racing by nearly out of breath. He sped past the Sweetwater wagon and off into the clearing behind them.

Two wagons behind, Jake Crawford galloped up the trail with a large coiled rope at his side. "Hemp justice! That's what we need around here! A little hemp justice!" Jake's voice boomed as he passed the Sweetwater wagon. He broke off to the right and his men followed in his dusty wake.

"Hemp justice? What's that?" Margaret asked Daniel.

"I don't know," Daniel replied.

A commotion erupted in the clearing. Jake and his men had surrounded William and closed in on him rapidly. Daniel climbed down and walked to the edge of the trail.

Jake's men had dismounted. William Dawes lay face down in the grass. Two men sat on him; two others tied his hands behind his back.

Frightened, Daniel stepped toward the group. Trembling on the inside, he called out. "What's going on here?"

Jake jerked his head around to see who was there. His stubborn eyes met Daniel's. "This is none of your business, boy! Get back to your wagon. Now!"

Daniel flinched but stood his ground. He felt someone brush up against his arm. He turned to find Margaret standing beside him, the blanket still wrapped around her. Her words startled him.

"Mr. Crawford, what are you doing?"

Jake stood, allowing his men to finish the job. Removing his hat, he strode boldly toward the two. "Miss Muhlenberg, we had a little problem early this morning. Dawes here was smokin' some of his weed last night. Caught one of the supply wagons on fire. Lost a month's worth of supplies due to his carelessness. But we got matters under control. Go on about your business."

Margaret persisted. "What are you going to do with him?"

"That's not for you to worry about."

Before Margaret's father could even step up to her side, Jake motioned him away.

"Just go on back to your wagon. Justice will be served. Anyone objecting can just pull out of the train right now." Without further explanation he turned back to his men.

William Dawes stood, his hands tied behind his back. The group circled him, kicking dust in his face, spitting on him and calling him names.

Margaret and Daniel climbed back aboard his wagon. There was nothing they could do and Daniel knew it. Crawford had everybody on the trail living in fear.

Daniel sat and seethed, staring into the cold January sky, his angry eyes ablaze with hatred. His hand dropped to his knife, and he gripped the handle tightly.

The long line of wagons began to move slowly. Daniel snapped the reins. Jake and his men sauntered up the trail, whooping and hollering. They had looped a hangman's noose around William Dawes' neck and attached the other end to Crawford's saddle. With his hands tied behind him, Dawes sprinted madly behind Crawford to keep from being dragged by the neck.

"Hemp justice! A little hemp justice!" Crawford bellowed again as the gang clipped by. His men laughed and shouted.

The group broke off to the left, toward a stand of trees. They stopped and dismounted. Dawes was lifted up onto Crawford's horse, the noose still around his neck. The rope was thrown over a branch and knotted.

The wagons kept moving and heads turned to watch the grisly spectacle.

Jake turned away from his men and called out to the slowly moving line. "This man's carelessness has cost you a month's worth of supplies. Your supplies!"

Crawford nodded his head. One of his men slapped the rump of the horse. Several pistols were fired into the air. The men shouted. The horse bolted away and Dawes slid off, suspended helplessly beneath the tree.

Daniel turned his head and shielded Margaret's eyes from the horrible sight.

"William didn't start that fire!" Daniel exclaimed, his fists tightening around the reins. He breathed heavily, anger rising within him. He turned his tortured face toward Margaret.

"I went to see William early this morning, just before breakfast. He was sleeping under a tree, fifty feet away. When I got there, I saw two of Jake's men smoking cigars. They were fumbling with something in William's wagon. I don't think they saw me, and I didn't say anything."

Few words were spoken that day. But secretly, silently, Daniel made his plans to end Crawford's treachery.

That night, as usual, Daniel ate with the Muhlenbergs. Dinner was cold. Daniel said goodnight and returned to his wagon.

From her stool near the fire, Margaret watched him walk away. As he passed by, she said, "Daniel, the Lord is faithful in his judgments. Eventually, the wicked become ensnared by the works of their own hands."

Daniel walked away in silence. The hour was late, but Daniel did not turn in. He sat on his blanket in the darkness, coldly calculating his next move.

13
THE KNIFE

The time had come. Daniel stood up. All along the trail, lanterns were being extinguished. He checked his knife carefully, adjusting the sheath on his belt. Crossing the clearing to his left, he reached the edge of the woods. Keeping his eyes on the wagons, he stole silently along the edge of the forest, his hot breath trailing behind in thin white puffs.

A hundred yards away in a clearing below, Daniel saw the glow of a campfire. He moved quietly toward its light. Men's laughter and loud chatter arose from the clearing. He listened carefully. Then he recognized the voice he wanted to hear.

Crawford!

Daniel crossed to the other side of the trail. Between each wagon, he could see the campfire getting closer. The voices grew louder. His heart pounded wildly.

He came within twenty feet of the men. Their loud voices continued to fill the cold night air. They had not seen him.

From the cover of the woods, Daniel dropped to his stomach and looked beneath the wagon. He saw Crawford from behind, leaning against a wagon wheel, his face partially lit by the campfire's light. He held a bottle in his left hand as the other hand slowly rubbed his holstered pistol.

"It's been a long time since we've had that kind of fun, eh boys?" Crawford bellowed, downing a swig from his bottle.

"Yeah, Jake, it was a great idea you had, settin' that wagon on fire." More coarse laughter filled the air.

"Did you see that old boy's face when we pulled out the noose?"

Gruff laughter erupted again.

"Charlie, where'd you stash all the supplies we stole before you torched the wagon?" Jake asked.

"Stuffed 'em in our wagons, of course." More laughter.

Daniel's surging hatred was stronger than his fear. So what if he died? He just wanted to kill Jake Crawford.

He lay quietly on his belly beneath the trees. He clenched the knife. Coarse talking and laughter continued for another hour. As he remained still in the cold grass, his heavy breathing subsided and a chill came over him. He fought to keep his teeth from chattering.

Slowly, one by one, Jake's men dropped off to sleep. At last, Crawford was the only man still by the fire. He sat quietly, leaning against the wagon wheel. Now and then, he lifted the bottle to his lips and took a drink. From the side, Daniel could see his face. Crawford belched.

Finally, Jake's hand let loose of the bottle and flopped to his side. Daniel watched as Crawford's head tilted backward against the wheel.

Daniel's heart began to pound again. Carefully, he inched toward Crawford. He stopped for a moment and listened.

Jake snored loudly.

It's now or never! Daniel inched forward. After several minutes, he reached the wagon. He stopped again, looked and listened carefully.

Jake continued to snore.

Daniel started crawling again. Under the wagon, he stopped. No one moved around the campfire's flickering remains. He scooted the rest of the way and lay silently two feet from Crawford—the man responsible for his father's death!

He raised his knife, edging ever closer to Crawford's exposed throat. Daniel took a breath as he moved the knife to Crawford's face. He felt Jake's hot breath on his hand. Daniel closed his eyes and swallowed hard.

From somewhere in the back of his mind, Harlan Smith's words rose and pierced Daniel's conscience. "Livin' on the frontier drives a man to choose which way he'll go—good or bad."

Daniel scrunched his lips together and fought to keep Harlan's words out, but to no avail.

"If to good, you'll be a wiser, better man. If to bad, you'll end up killin' before it's over."

The knife wavered precariously two inches above Jake's neck. Daniel pictured himself standing next to his father at Robert Muskrat's gravesite. He clenched his teeth and pressed the knife closer. Only a thin space separated the edge of the knife from Jake's throat.

Harlan's honest face returned to his thoughts. Was Harlan right? Did he really want to become just like the man he sought desperately to kill? Did he want to become like Jake Crawford?

His hunger for revenge fluttered, then faded altogether.

He slowly withdrew the knife from Crawford's neck. He knelt motionless for several moments. How he hated him! But he could not do this deed, not if it meant becoming like Crawford!

Then a chill crept over him. What if Crawford awoke and discovered him under the wagon? How could he possibly explain his presence there with an unsheathed knife?

Crawford stirred. His eyelids fluttered.

Daniel stifled a cry, but inside, he screamed. God, help me!

Jake folded his hands across his chest, muttered to himself, then began noisily sucking air through his mouth.

Drained of strength, Daniel edged himself away. As he passed under the backside of the wagon, he stopped and listened. All was quiet except for his breathing and Jake's snores. He rested a moment, knife in hand, then continued crawling backward in the direction of the trees. After many torturous minutes filled with night sounds that would stop him in his tracks, the heel of his boot finally rustled the underbrush.

He'd made it!

Coated with dirt and suddenly chilled to the bone, Daniel climbed cautiously to his feet. He started to walk, then broke into a run toward his wagon.

At last he reached the glowing remains of his campfire. Despair crashed down heavily upon him. He collapsed to his knees beneath the vast, black sky, and wept.

14

THE LETTER

The Cherokee people reached their destination on the first day of March. From Ellijay, Georgia, to Fort Gibson, Oklahoma, they had wound a thousand miles through the mountains and valleys of Tennessee, Kentucky, Illinois, Missouri and Arkansas. After traveling through the depth of winter, nearly a hundred bodies had been left behind in shallow graves. The Cherokee relocation had been a grim trail of tears filled with suffering and death.

Daniel sat somberly by the remains of the campfire. Frost covered the tall grass outside the fire circle and the wagons. Today would be his last day to spend with Margaret. Tomorrow, the Muhlenberg family would head north for Shawnee Mission, Kansas. By law he would stay behind with the Cherokees.

Other than meeting Harlan Smith, the old frontiersman and first white man he had ever liked, his friendship with Margaret was the only good thing to come from the long journey. She was strong, full of faith and wisdom. She cared, not only about him, but also about his people. He had learned many things from her. His untrusting heart had softened because of her persistent pursuit of friendship.

Daniel sighed. She was leaving, and they would never see each other again. Up until now, he had not realized just how much he cared for her.

Margaret climbed down from the wagon. "Daniel, what's this Bible with the hole in it?"

Daniel looked from the Bible in her hands to the gray, cloud-strewn sky.

He remembered the last day before their miserable trek west had begun. Angry and resentful, he had challenged God that day, raising his fist and shaking it at him—the same day Crawford shot his father.

"It's a long story, Margaret. I don't want to go into it now." Another picture formed in his mind. Daniel saw his knife inch its way toward Jake Crawford's exposed neck. A chill slid down his spine. He didn't want to get into a discussion that might lead to Margaret discovering that he'd almost murdered Jake Crawford.

"All right," she answered as she opened the Bible. "But did you know you have a letter from your father stuck inside?" Margaret sat on her campstool beside Daniel. She handed him the letter, then wrapped a blanket around her legs.

Margaret leaned forward and ladled herself a cup of soup from the pot hanging over the fire.

"It's dated the day before. . ." Daniel hesitated, swallowing hard and fighting back sudden tears. "The day before he died."

Margaret's eyes widened. "Read it, Daniel," she said, softly.

"I can't," he replied slowly, handing the letter back to her.

Margaret set her cup of soup on the ground beside her. The March wind snapped at her blanket, blowing it up around her legs. She took a breath, turned on her stool to capture the fire-light on the face of the letter and began to read.

> *Dear Daniel,*
>
> *Since the afternoon that Jake Crawford shot me in the shoulder, you and I have had few words between us. There are many things I wish to share with you, but your anger has blinded your heart. So, I am writing you a letter now, trusting that God will find the moment for me to give this to you.*
>
> *The night that Jake Crawford whipped Robert Muskrat, I was about to tell you the story of your grandfather Jacob. This letter will tell you that story. Your grandfather Jacob, my father, was seven years old when he lost his family in the Ohio wilderness. His father, Netawatwees, your great-grandfather, was chief of the*

Delaware Moravian tribe. Netawatwees had converted to Christianity five years earlier and took the name Abraham. He had led his people to the Way of the Cross.

It was in March of 1782 that Abraham and his people were forced to leave their homelands as the white man came and claimed their land. There was great violence in those days, on both sides, red and white, and tribes could be slaughtered if they refused to move.

Abraham accepted protection from Colonel Williamson who directed the Delawares to follow him to Fort Pitt, Pennsylvania.

Abraham trusted Colonel Williamson because only the year before, other Delawares had been treated well and given many gifts at Fort Pitt. At Williamson's request, Abraham told his people it was safe to surrender their arms.

Shortly after their journey out of their home at Gnaddenhutten near the Tuscarawas River, Abraham's people found themselves encircled by white men leveling rifles at them. To Abraham's dismay, Williamson ordered them bound.

The Delaware were led back to their own camp and placed in two large buildings which were actually mission rooms that they had built for their worship services. The men were taken into one building, the women and children into the other. In all, ninety-eight Delaware Moravians were made to sit on the floor with their feet bound.

The next morning Williamson and his men decided that their captives should be executed. Abraham told Williamson that his people were innocent but were prepared to die if that was what God had ordained. He requested Williamson to grant him and his people one night to pray and repent of their sins and to make themselves right with God. Williamson agreed.

That night, many tears were shed as wailing and moaning filled the two rooms.

Morning came. Twenty of Williamson's soldiers entered the building that held the Delaware men. One of Williamson's captains led the group. Without saying a word, he raised a large mallet and smashed your great-grandfather Abraham's skull. The captain pulled his knife, took Abraham's scalp and let out a whoop. The captain continued, felling thirteen more. A second soldier took the next turn, felling eleven. And so it went until every Delaware in the room was dead.

Next door, similar sounds could be heard. One of Williamson's men assigned to the women and children's building could not stomach the violence. He ran out of the room to vomit, leaving the door ajar. Three boys, who throughout the night had worked their bonds free, made their escape. They bolted out the door and into the dark forest. They were the only survivors of this horrible massacre.

As you can probably now conclude, Jacob, your grandfather, was one of the boys. They ran seven miles to Schoenbrun, warning other Delaware Moravians of Williamson's treachery.

For many years, Jacob fought back a growing root of bitterness and hatred. By God's grace, his love and obedience to God defeated the darkness inside him. Learning to forgive, he grew into a man of God. All of his days, he lived by the Moravian creed, "Whether by life or death, Christ be glorified."

Your grandfather loved you very much. He believed that God has a special calling for your life, one that will bring hope and justice to all the native nations.

Daniel, do you remember when I told you that we are Christians first, Moravians second, and Delaware third? The Moravians have a symbol that also represents their creed. It is an altar and a yoked oxen: to die or to serve. Daniel, we must always be ready for either.

I do not know how our journey will end. We have

witnessed many terrors of our own these last bitter months. Please consider the testimony of your great-grandfather Abraham and your grandfather Jacob. I love you, my son.

"Signed, 'Your father, Thomas.' " Margaret looked up, tears rolling down her cheeks. Daniel wept, his elbows propped on his knees, his face buried in his hands. His body trembled; his shoulders rose and fell. The deep sobs sprang from the center of his soul.

She wiped away her tears with the sleeve of her coat, then moved closer and wrapped his blanket tighter around him.

"Daniel, you have such a rich heritage of faith."

They sat quietly for several moments. The wind picked up and a bright, golden curve of sun appeared from behind the edge of the clouds.

Margaret broke the silence. The sadness around her eyes melted away, revealing a glint of inspiration.

"Daniel, you never told me that you were a Delaware. I always thought that you were a Cherokee, like the people we were traveling with."

"I never thought much about it," he replied, rubbing his eyes and sniffling.

Margaret grinned. "You know, this gives me an idea. Let's go talk to my father."

15

TRUTH

Twenty minutes later, Daniel, Margaret and Peter stood in the small office of Colonel Samuel Burns, one of the officers in charge of Fort Gibson and the Cherokee resettlement in Oklahoma.

He reread the letter resting on his desk. He nodded his head and rubbed his chin.

"I agree with your assessment, Reverend Muhlenberg. This letter appears genuine. I will accept your proposition that Daniel is a Delaware, not a Cherokee, and is therefore not under the government's jurisdiction. He is free to leave with you for Shawnee Mission. On the other hand, knowing of his father's honorable role with the Cherokee people, I have no problem if he chooses to stay."

No sooner had Colonel Burns spoken, than the door to his office burst open, startling everyone.

Jake Crawford stormed through the door. "What's this I hear about the Indian?" he bellowed, his hand lowered to his pistol.

Colonel Burns stood up, red-faced. "Mr. Crawford, this matter no longer concerns you. I have received written reports of your conduct on the trail. I will be investigating these reports to determine if any action can and should be taken against you. I suggest you leave my office immediately or be placed under arrest."

The colonel tugged firmly at the jacket of his uniform. "In my opinion, Daniel's people have seen enough injustice for a lifetime. I order you to stay away from them."

Two armed soldiers stepped through the open door behind Crawford.

Crawford looked over his shoulder, then relaxed his stance.

He glared at Daniel, but said nothing. He pushed the soldiers aside and left the office.

Colonel Burns returned the letter to Daniel. "As I said, you're free to go. Good luck."

That evening, Peter stood behind his daughter who sat on her stool by Daniel's fire.

Daniel reached behind him and picked up another log. The proud Delaware tossed the log into the fire and stoked the flames high and bright.

"You see Daniel, God is just," Peter explained, his hands on Margaret's shoulders. "He uses His own means to bring about His judgment in His due time. Sometimes He will use those in authority over us. We must never take things into our own hands. We must let God be God. We can only hope and pray that the investigation will find Jake Crawford guilty of his crimes and that justice will prevail."

Having spoken, Peter Muhlenberg nodded and stepped away, leaving Margaret and Daniel alone. He climbed into the back of his nearby wagon. Little Mary waved at Daniel before her father's hands pulled her away from the covered opening.

Daniel smiled and folded his hands. He had lost his father and many friends. He had made some bad choices and had learned many lessons, but good things had happened, too. He had met Margaret. And tomorrow, he would be leaving with her, Mary and their family for Shawnee Mission and a fresh start with hope in his heart.

And finally he knew—not just within himself—but that others no longer considered him a boy, but a man.

As the two talked quietly, the sound of a horse's hoofs pounding on hard ground grew louder.

Margaret looked at Daniel. "Who would that be, coming up so swiftly?"

Without warning, Jake Crawford rode his prancing, snorting steed into the wide circle of flickering firelight.

He leaned forward in the saddle and stared viciously at Daniel, his mouth twisted into a grotesque, hateful sneer. He yanked his pistol from his holster, its barrel gleaming red and orange from the fire.

Margaret rose to her feet and put her hands to her mouth.

Crawford aimed the barrel straight between Daniel's eyes.

"I should just kill you right here and now, savage!"

With a loud click, Crawford cocked the gun's hammer with his thumb.

Daniel stood up. Courage rose from deep inside him, from the center of his heart.

He took a step toward Crawford. At first, words from his father, Harlan Smith, and Peter leapt into his thoughts: whether by life or death; Christ be glorified; to die or to serve.

But the words that came out of his mouth were words that had been spoken by the one person who now loved him more than any other.

Margaret's words were the very words that Jake Crawford needed to hear.

"The Lord is faithful in his judgments. Repent, Jake Crawford, or one day you will be ensnared by the works of your own hands."

Daniel held his ground.

Crawford's eyes glossed over.

Just like the day Thomas had declared that the world belonged to God and not to the white man, Crawford sat speechless on his horse. His lips curled upward, showing clenched teeth. His words were trapped in his mouth, bound by an invisible force.

He shuddered, his head snapping toward the darkness. With a noisy gurgle in his throat, he yanked hard on the reins. His horse neighed, eyes wide and nostrils flaring, and broke quickly away from the circle of light.

Daniel turned away and stepped over the stools.

He wrapped his arm around Margaret's shoulder. He lifted her trembling chin, then pointed up at the clear night sky. A million stars glimmered brightly, illuminating their upturned faces.

"I have endured injustice at the hands of white men, but I found kinship with an old frontiersman whose wisdom I shall never forget. I have lost my father, who gave his life to save another, but I found you, Margaret, and a love that will not let go. And though I have suffered, I now realize that God has a plan and a future for my life. I've been so slow to see. But finally, I understand."

Daniel smiled. "God was never angry with me at all!"

ADDITIONAL READING

The Cherokees

Claro, Nicole. *The Cherokee Indians*. Philadelphia: Chelsea House. Publishers. 1991.

Landau, Elaine. *The Cherokees*. New York: Franklin Watts. 1992.

Lepthien, Emilie U. *The Cherokee*. Chicago: Children's Press. 1992.

Woodward, Grace Steele. *The Cherokees*. Norman and London: University of Oklahoma Press. 1963.

The Cherokee Trail of Tears

Brill, Marlene Targ. *The Trail of Tears: The Cherokee Journey From Home*. Brookfield, Connecticut: The Millbrook Press, Inc. 1995.

Bealer, Alex W. *Only the Names Remain: The Cherokees and the Trail of Tears*. Boston: Little, Brown and Company. 1972.

Williams, Jeanne. *Trails of Tears: American Indians Driven from Their Lands*. Dallas: Hendrick-Long Publishing Co. 1992.

The Delaware (Lenni Lenape)

Grumet, Robert S. *The Lenapes*. New York: Chelsea House Publishers. 1989.

Miller, Jay. *The Delaware*. Chicago: Children's Press. 1994.

Lenni Lenape Historical Society & Museum (on the Internet). http://www.lenape.org/main.html

European / Indian Relations

Prucha, Francis Paul. *The Indians in American Society: From the Revolutionary War to the Present*. Los Angeles: University of California Press. 1985.

Calloway, Colin G. (Editor). *The World Turned Upside Down: Indian Voices from Early America*. Boston: Bedford Books of St. Martin's Press. 1994.

The Moravians

Mitchell, Barbara. *Tomahawks and Trombones*. Minneapolis: Carolrhoda Books. 1982.

Sawyer, Edwin A. *All About the Moravians: History, Beliefs, and Practices of a Worldwide Church*. Winston-Salem: The Moravian Church in America. 1992.

Trappers and Trapping

O'Neill, Paul. *The Frontiersmen: The Old West*. Alexandria, Virginia: Time-Life Books. 1977.

Simms, Jeptha R. *Trappers of New York*. Harrison, New York: Harbor Hill Books. 1980.

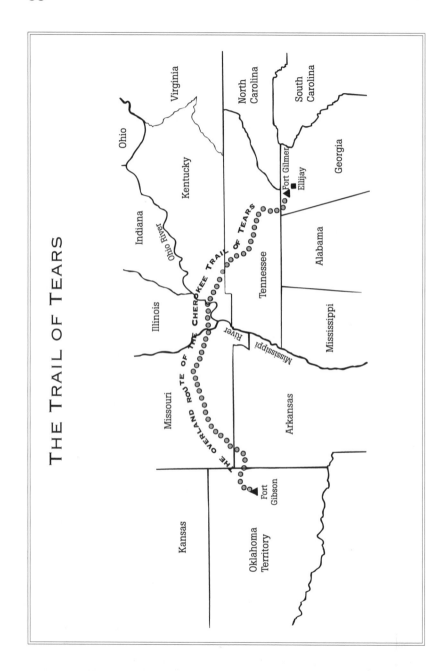

THE TRAIL OF TEARS

THE CHEROKEE NATION
AND THE TRAIL OF TEARS

The Cherokee people hold a unique place in American history. In early colonial times, many Cherokees married British traders. From these marriage unions, prosperous, mixed blood families emerged who eventually sided with the British during the Revolutionary War.

Following the war, the Cherokee people lived quietly in Georgia, North Carolina and Tennessee. Because they had sided with the British, they struggled to gain favor with the newly formed government. Establishing communities much like the whites of that era, Cherokees lived in frame and brick houses, cultivated fields and raised poultry and hogs. They developed agricultural skills. They also became adept in spinning and weaving. The Cherokee people actually became more civilized than many whites of that generation.

Sequoyah, a mixed blood Cherokee, developed the Cherokee alphabet and the Cherokees became the first native American tribe to read and write in their own language. They adopted their first written law in 1808.

The first Methodist Mission School was established in 1801 and Methodist circuit riding preachers began holding meetings on Cherokee tribal lands in 1822. Many Cherokees became Christians.

Between 1785 and 1902, twenty-five separate treaties were made between the US government and the Cherokee people. Of these twenty-five, eighteen provided for the surrender of tribal Cherokee land to the U.S. government.

In 1798, the Treaty of Tiello between the Cherokee and the U.S. promised that 43,000 square miles of tribal Cherokee land would be Cherokee "forever." That same year gold was discovered on Cherokee land.

In spite of treaties and promises, many Cherokees sensed the newly formed and developing nation would provide them little chance of maintaining their communities. Many began moving voluntarily. In the face of the coming European tide, 3,000 relocated to Arkansas by 1815 and 7,000 by 1817.

Even as early as 1794 President George Washington had written to the Cherokee leaders and explained that more than 10,000 white people were already inhabiting Cherokee lands and could not be removed. Several presidential terms later, President Martin Van Buren expressed the general attitude of the nation when he proclaimed that "no state can achieve proper culture, civilization and progress in safety as long as Indians are permitted to remain."

Many Cherokees were Christians. Oddly, the Cherokee people often proved to be more civilized and educated than many of the whites who were slowly encroaching upon their tribal lands. As the press for removal began in earnest, Cherokee leaders lobbied Washington to remain. To justify their actions, whites portrayed the Cherokee people as primitive, savage, heathen—ideas which simply were not based in truth.

In 1830, Congress passed the Removal Bill, allocating money for negotiating a buyout of Cherokee tribal lands. But the Cherokee cause was defended by many including Noah Webster, John Adams, Sam Houston (an adopted Cherokee) and Davy Crockett.

The Cherokee people began to divide over the issue of the removal and many of the mixed blood Cherokee felt that their cause held little hope. They began advocating a mass move westward and the acceptance of the government's terms. Still, most Cherokees refused to believe that they would ever be removed from the land of their heritage.

The mixed bloods led by Major Ridge and known as the Treaty Party made an agreement with the government. But the vast majority of the Cherokees led by Chief John Ross refused to accept the validity of Ridge's agreement.

Meanwhile, Ridge and his followers moved west and resettled. But around 15,000 Cherokee remained on their land, determined to stay. As the May, 1838 deadline approached, the deadline imposed by Ridge's treaty, President Van Buren assigned General Winfield Scott the responsibility of removing the Cherokee.

Few came voluntarily. Scott's 4,000 regulars and 3,000 volunteers were ordered to forcibly remove the Cherokee nation. Still holding out hope that Chief Ross would work everything out for them, most Cherokees were not ready to leave their homes.

The Cherokee were snatched up from their dinner tables or from their work in the fields with no warning, as the Army corralled and herded them into four separate detention camps. Ill prepared, most lost their lifetime belongings.

The Cherokee began their one thousand mile trek to Oklahoma. The "Trail of Tears" as it has come to be known proved a deadly journey. Uprooted from their native homeland, forced against their will, heartbroken, filled with despair and ravaged with disease, many Cherokees expired along the way. Of the 13,000 people forcibly removed from their tribal homelands, 4,000 died en route to Oklahoma.

The story told in Thomas' letter of the Delaware chief Netawatwees, the Delaware Moravians and their massacre by Colonel Williamson's army at Gnadenhutten is true: two young boys did escape as described. However, the third boy, Jacob, is fictionalized.

Today, most Cherokees live in Oklahoma. They are full citizens of the United States and continue to possess great pride in their native culture and heritage.

[1] Martin Van Buren as quoted in *Trails of Tears* by Jeanne Williams p.158